EXPLORE THE U.S.A.

NEW MEXICO

Cindy Rodriguez

LET'S READ
AV²
BY WEIGL
ADDED VALUE • AUDIO VISUAL

www.av2books.com

Go to **www.av2books.com**, and enter this book's unique code.

BOOK CODE

P 5 5 4 2 2 7

AV² by Weigl brings you media enhanced books that support active learning.

AV² provides enriched content that supplements and complements this book. Weigl's AV² books strive to create inspired learning and engage young minds in a total learning experience.

Your AV² Media Enhanced books come alive with...

Audio
Listen to sections of the book read aloud.

Video
Watch informative video clips.

Embedded Weblinks
Gain additional information for research.

Try This!
Complete activities and hands-on experiments.

Key Words
Study vocabulary, and complete a matching word activity.

Quizzes
Test your knowledge.

Slide Show
View images and captions, and prepare a presentation.

... and much, much more!

Published by AV² by Weigl
350 5th Avenue, 59th Floor
New York, NY 10118
Website: www.av2books.com   www.weigl.com

Library of Congress Cataloging-in-Publication Data
Rodriguez, Cindy.
 New Mexico / Cindy Rodriguez.
   p. cm. -- (Explore the U.S.A.)
 Includes bibliographical references and index.
 ISBN 978-1-61913-381-5 (hard cover : alk. paper)
 1. New Mexico--Juvenile literature. I. Title.
 F796.3.R63 2013
 978.9--dc23
                            2012015607

Printed in the United States of America in North Mankato, Minnesota
1 2 3 4 5 6 7 8 9   16 15 14 13 12

052012
WEP040512

Project Coordinator: Karen Durrie
Art Director: Terry Paulhus

Weigl acknowledges Getty Images as the primary image supplier for this title.

NEW MEXICO

Contents

3

This is New Mexico.
It is called the Land of Enchantment.
New Mexico has very beautiful landscapes.

This is the shape of New Mexico. It is in the south part of the United States.

Where is New Mexico?

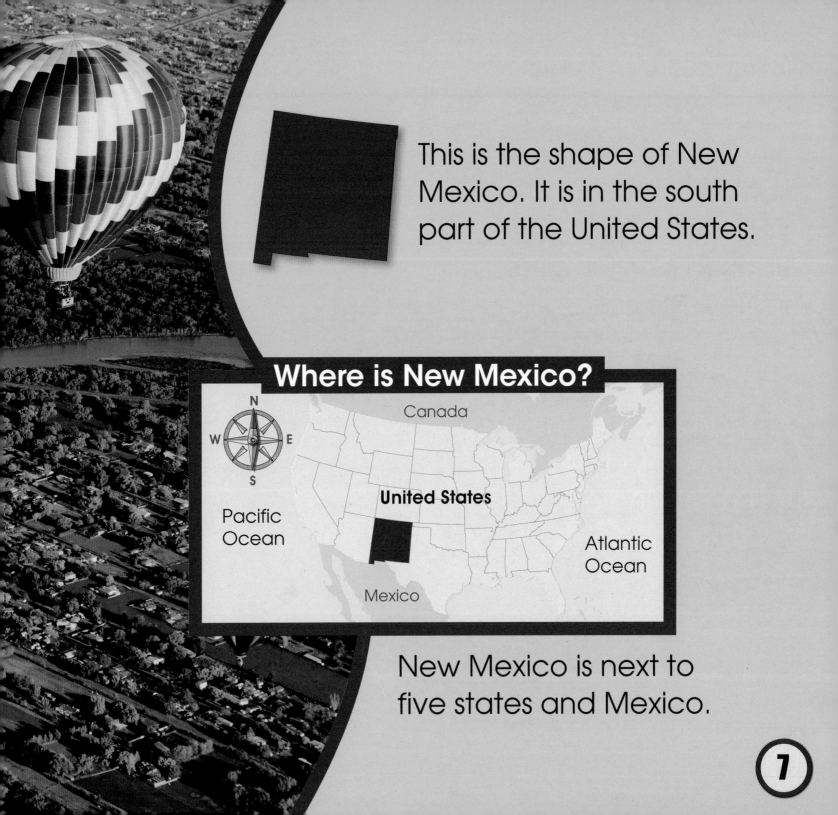

Canada

N
W · E
S

Pacific Ocean

United States

Atlantic Ocean

Mexico

New Mexico is next to five states and Mexico.

New Mexico had many early settlers. American Indians, Latin Americans, and Spanish people all settled in New Mexico.

Many houses in New Mexico look like early Pueblo Indian houses.

The yucca is the New Mexico state flower. This white flower blooms in spring and has very sharp leaves.

The New Mexico state seal has a large American eagle on top of a smaller Mexican eagle.

The Mexican eagle holds a snake and a cactus.

This is the state flag of New Mexico. The flag is red and yellow with a sun in the middle.

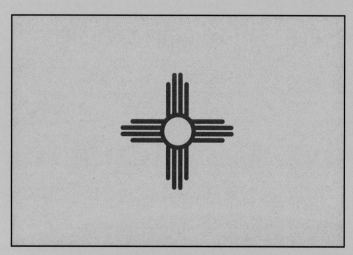

The sun on the flag is called a Zia.

The state animal of New Mexico is the black bear. Black bears are not always black. They can be many different colors.

Black bears eat nuts, berries, and insects.

The capital of New Mexico is Santa Fe. Santa Fe is the oldest capital city in the United States.

The Santa Fe Trail is 900 miles long.

17

New Mexico is known for its American Indian crafts. Many groups of people in New Mexico have their own kinds of art.

New Mexico is also known for its Spanish art.

Albuquerque, New Mexico, is known around the world for its hot air balloon festival. It is the largest festival of this kind in the world.

NEW MEXICO FACTS

These pages provide detailed information that expands on the interesting facts found in the book. These pages are intended to be used by adults as a learning support to help young readers round out their knowledge of each state in the *Explore the U.S.A.* series.

Pages 4–5

New Mexico's nickname comes from its varied culture and natural beauty. The American Indians, Spanish, and Mexicans all create arts and crafts representing their unique traditions. New Mexico is home to the Rocky Mountains and the Badland's dry lava plains. It also has the Rio Grande, hot springs, and scorching desert areas. New Mexico is the fifth largest state in the United States.

Pages 6–7

On January 6, 1912, New Mexico joined the United States as the 47th state. Its neighbors are Colorado to the north and Oklahoma and Texas to the east. Arizona is to the west, and the two Mexican states of Chihuahua and Sonora are on New Mexico's southwest border. New Mexico is one of the Four Corners, along with Utah, Arizona, and Colorado. It is the only place in the United States where four states meet at one point.

Pages 8–9

Some of the first American Indians in this area were the people of the Mogollon culture. Next came the Anasazi, who were the ancestors of today's Pueblo Indians. The Navajo and Apache settled in the area during the 1400s. In the 1500s, the Spanish became the first European explorers in this region.

Pages 10–11

The yucca was selected as the state flower in 1927. It is a symbol of sturdiness and beauty. The Mexican eagle grasping a snake and cactus on the seal represents the importance of New Mexico's Spanish, Mexican, and American Indian traditions. The larger American eagle symbolizes the U.S. protection of New Mexico and the state's heritage and culture.

Red and yellow are the colors of Spain's flag. They have been the colors of the New Mexico flag since 1925. The sun symbol Zia stands for the four directions and four seasons. It also stands for the four parts of the day—sunrise, noon, evening, and night—and the four parts of life—childhood, youth, middle age, and old age.

The New Mexico black bear is a subspecies of the American black bear. Black bears are found across North America. They can be black, brown, cinnamon, or even white. Black bears can be up to 6 feet (1.8 meters) long and weigh more than 600 pounds (270 kilograms). Their home range can cover 80 square miles (200 square kilometers).

When the Mexican-American War ended in 1848, Mexico gave land to the United States. This included what is now New Mexico. The U.S. Territory of New Mexico was established in 1850. New Mexico's capital city, Santa Fe, is the end point of the 900-mile (1,450-kilometer) Santa Fe Trail.

Folk arts are the traditional arts passed down through a specific cultural group. Folk art reflects the values of the groups that make it. This art also helps spread and preserve New Mexico's history and cultural heritage. Sante Fe is home to the Museum of International Folk Art. It houses the world's largest collection of folk art.

Visitors are attracted to the many activities available in New Mexico. Albuquerque boasts 310 days of sunshine and light winds each year, making it perfect for hot air ballooning. Angel Fire is a famous ski resort located in the Sangre de Cristo Mountains. Carlsbad Caverns has more than 100 caves people can explore.

KEY WORDS

Research has shown that as much as 65 percent of all written material published in English is made up of 300 words. These 300 words cannot be taught using pictures or learned by sounding them out. They must be recognized by sight. This book contains 53 common sight words to help young readers improve their reading fluency and comprehension. This book also teaches young readers several important content words, such as proper nouns. These words are paired with pictures to aid in learning and improve understanding.

Page	Sight Words First Appearance
4	has, is, it, land, of, the, this, very
7	and, in, next, part, states, to, where
8	all, American, had, houses, Indians, like, look, many, people
11	a, large, leaves, on, white
12	with
15	always, animal, are, be, can, different, eat, not, they
16	city, long, miles
19	also, for, groups, have, its, kinds, their, own
21	air, around, world

Page	Content Words First Appearance
4	enchantment, landscapes, New Mexico
7	Mexico, shape, United States
8	Latin Americans, settlers, towns
11	cactus, eagle, flower, seal, snake, spring, yucca
12	flag, Sun, Zia
15	berries, black bear, colors, insects, nuts
16	capital, Sante Fe, Sante Fe Trail
19	art, crafts
21	Albuquerque, balloon, festival

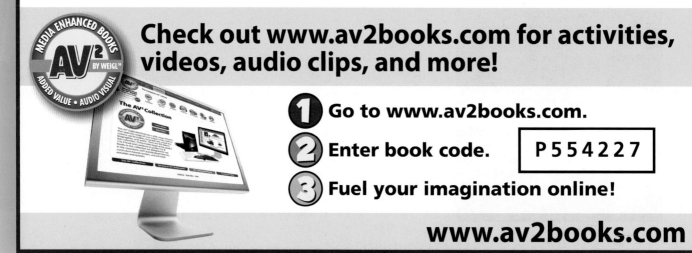

Check out www.av2books.com for activities, videos, audio clips, and more!

1 Go to www.av2books.com.

2 Enter book code. P554227

3 Fuel your imagination online!

www.av2books.com